Unusual Pets of Presidents

Grace Hansen

Abdo Kids Junior
is an Imprint of Abdo Kids
abdobooks.com

abdobooks.com

Published by Abdo Kids, a division of ABDO, P.O. Box 398166, Minneapolis, Minnesota 55439.

Printed in the United States of America, North Mankato, Minnesota.

102021

012022

THIS BOOK CONTAINS RECYCLED MATERIALS

Photo Credits: Library of Congress, Shutterstock, Smithsonian Archives

Production Contributors: Teddy Borth, Jennie Forsberg, Grace Hansen

Design Contributors: Candice Keimig, Pakou Moua

Library of Congress Control Number: 2021939929

Publisher's Cataloging-in-Publication Data

Names: Hansen, Grace, author.

Title: Unusual pets of presidents / by Grace Hansen

Description: Minneapolis, Minnesota : Abdo Kids, 2022 | Series: Pets of presidents | Includes online resources and index.

Identifiers: ISBN 9781098209285 (lib. bdg.) | ISBN 9781644946930 (pbk.) | ISBN 9781098209988 (ebook) | ISBN 9781098260347 (Read-to-Me ebook)

Subjects: LCSH: Exotic animals--Juvenile literature. | Pets--Juvenile literature. | Presidents--Juvenile literature. | Presidents' pets--United States--Juvenile literature.

Classification: DDC 973--dc23

Table of Contents

Unusual Pets of Presidents

Almost every US president has had pets. Some have had very unusual pets!

Thomas Jefferson was gifted two grizzly bear cubs. He knew he could not keep them. They went to a new home.

Thomas Jefferson

John Quincy Adams had an alligator. He kept it in a White House bathtub. It was soon sent to a better place.

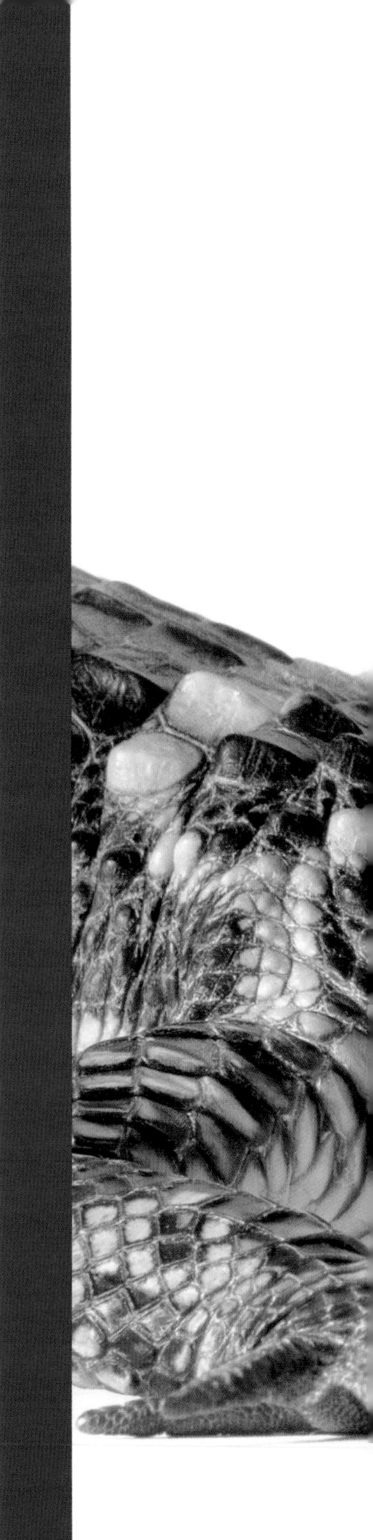

John Quincy Adams

The Roosevelts had many pets. The family had a flying squirrel. They also had a snake.

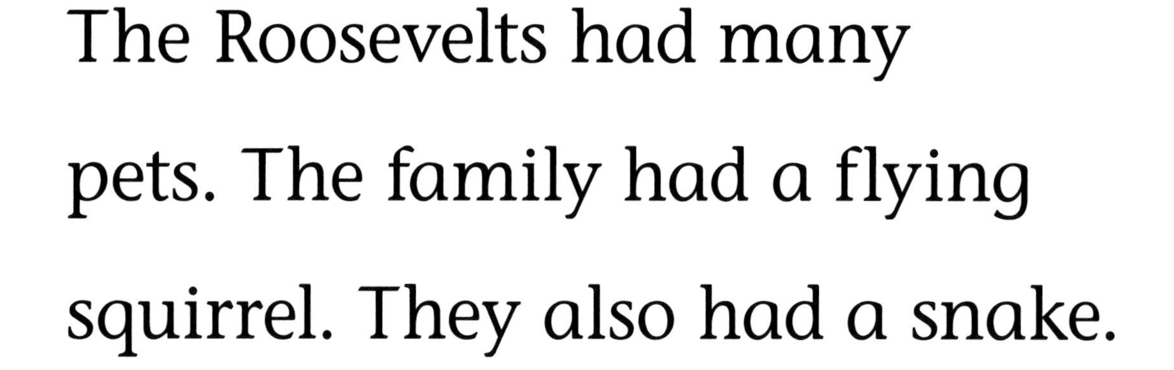

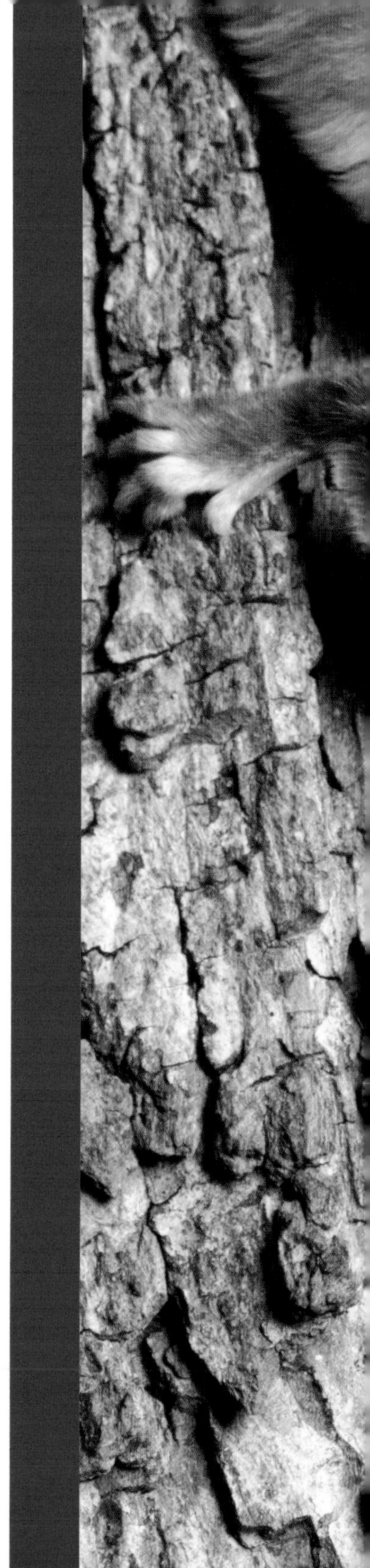

Theodore Roosevelt and Family

The Roosevelts had two kangaroo rats. They also had Guinea pigs and much more!

Two presidents had squirrels named Pete. One played in the White House with Harding. The other walked with Truman.

Warren G. Harding

Harry S. Truman

Harding's Pete

The Coolidges had lots of pets too. They had two raccoons. Their names were Rebecca and Reuben.

Calvin Coolidge

Rebecca the raccoon

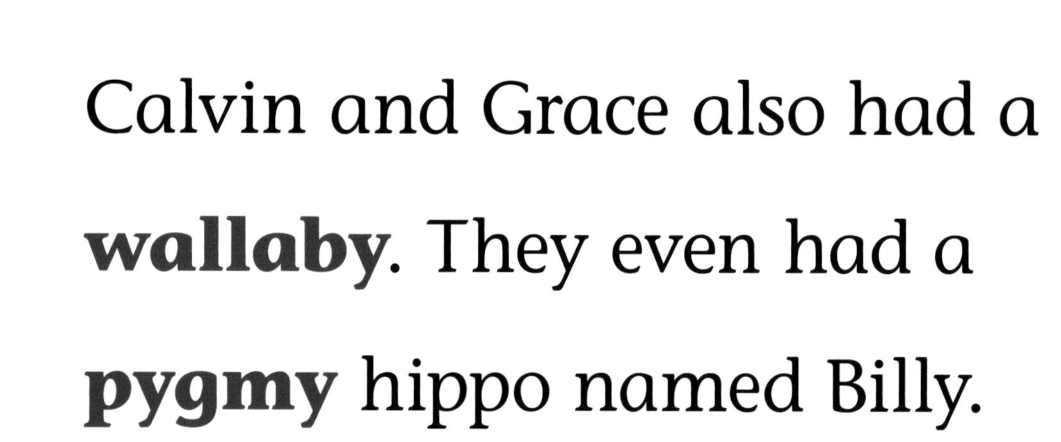

Calvin and Grace also had a **wallaby**. They even had a **pygmy** hippo named Billy.

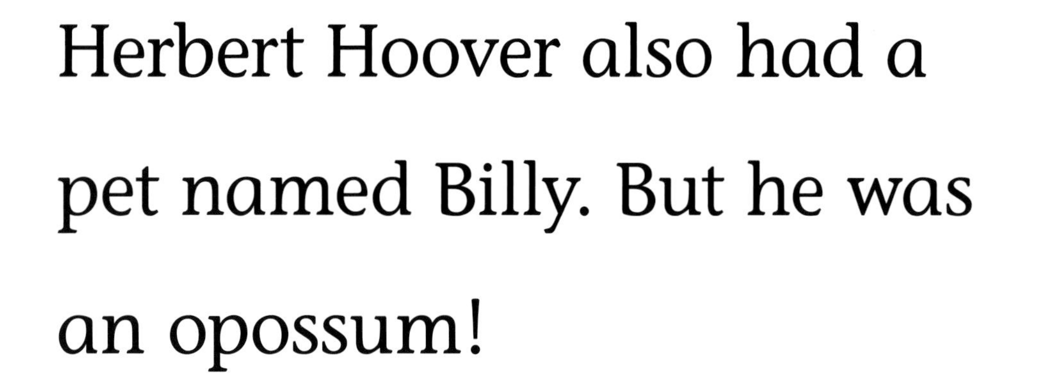

Herbert Hoover also had a pet named Billy. But he was an opossum!

Herbert Hoover

More First Pets

James Buchanan
elephant

Abraham Lincoln
Jack the turkey

Andrew Johnson
mice

Benjamin Harrison
Mr. Protection the opossum

Glossary

pygmy
something very small of its kind.

wallaby
any of various marsupials native to Australia and strongly resembling small or medium-sized kangaroos.

Index

Visit **abdokids.com** to access crafts, games, videos, and more!

Use Abdo Kids code

or scan this QR code!